Surviving Cameron Parish Records

Loudoun County Virginia

Tithable List of 1765

Abstracted by

June Whitehurst Johnson, CG

HERITAGE BOOKS
2019

HERITAGE BOOKS
AN IMPRINT OF HERITAGE BOOKS, INC.

Books, CDs, and more—Worldwide

For our listing of thousands of titles see our website
at
www.HeritageBooks.com

Published 2019 by
HERITAGE BOOKS, INC.
Publishing Division
5810 Ruatan Street
Berwyn Heights, Md. 20740

International Standard Book Number
Paperbound: 978-1-58549-709-6

PREFACE

The records that have been abstracted in this book were found in a suit in Loudoun County, Virginia, suit number M:2491 Lane & West vs Evans et als 1771. It was thought before the discovery of these records that none of the records of Cameron Parish were in existence , therefore it was most exciting to find these few documents.

The surviving records cover only a few years (1763-1767) and only a part of the parish. The area of the county covered is above Goose Creek and Little River to Fauquier County line. It appears in these records there is a tithable list for this district above Goose Creek and Little River for the year 1765.

Surviving Cameron Parish Records
Loudoun County, Virginia
Tithable list of 1765

John Evans, James Milton and John Andrews are bound unto William Carr Lane and George West, Gent. Church Wardens of Cameron Parish for the time being in full sum of 1000 lbs. current money of Virginia to be paid to sd. William Carr Lane and George West dated June 14, 1765.
The condition of the above obligation is such that were as the above bound John Evans hath under taken the collection of the Parish levey for the present year in the District above Goose Creek and Little River to the county line of Fauquire which collection he obliges him self to account for monthly upon the oath to the above sd. Lane & West one sixth part from the date here of what ever of the sd. collection shall be due and to settle and pay the whole agreeable to the list of tithables by the 25th day of Dec. next, also to settle upon oath with the vestry if required for all delinkquents agreeable to the arct. Assembly in that case made and provided, now if the sd. John Evans shall well and truty perform all and every covenants and article above mentioned then the above obligation to be void else to remain in full foce and virtue.

Jno. Andrews
Jas. Hamilton

Wits: Cha. Tyler, Chas. Binns
George the third of Great Britain, France and Irelan King Defender of the Faith, to the Sherif of Loudoun County greeting. We command you that you take John Andrews if he be found within your bailiwick, and safety keep so that you have his body before our Justices of sd. County Court on the second Monday in July next to answer William Carr Lane & Geo: West Churchwardens of Cameron Parish in a plea of debt for 1000 pounds current money of Virginia damages 100 pounds. And have then there this writ witness Charles Binns, Clerk of sd. court at courthouse 15th June 7th year of our reign 1767.

At Vestry held for Cameron Parish November 16, 1764 the Vestry proceeded this day to lay the levy as followith:

Pd. to:

Revd. John Andrews, his sallery	17120
Henry Willson clerk at Rockey Run	1200
John Lewis clerk at Broad Run Church	800
Thos. Lewis clerk Leesburg & Mt. "	2400
Charles Eskeridge sexton Rockey Run	400
John Piles sexton Broad Run Church	400
John Moss Jr. sexton Leesburg	400
John Harris sexton Mt. Church	400
Leven Powell clerk of the Vestry	500
Josias Clapham	400
Revd. John Andrews	84
Adam & Campbell	41
John Carlyle by acct. allow'd.	
William Ross	1136

```
John Moss by accot.                        300
Flem. Patterson                            748
William  Mead 4 levys over the  chd.
   in 1758                                  80
Benjamin Sebastia(n) 2 do last yr.          66
Charles Binns by accot.                    219
William Winn 2 levys overchd. last
   yr.                                      44
Charles Binns his judg't. over
   Church Wardens                          422
Robert Hamilton by accot.                   80
John Queen for support of Eliza.
   Powderall                              1500
Doctor John Urguhart by accot.             240
Craven Peyton by do.                       480
Elinor Coleman by do.                     1200
William Metheny for support of
   a child                                 800
William Carr Lane by accot.                210
Edwd. Thompson for support of Bryan
   Finnckan                                800
Tobacco levied for the use of the
   parish                                 4000
Henry Lander 1 levy over chd. last
   year                                     22
William Metheny 1 do.                       22
                                         36514

         6 pcr. for collecting           2190
                                         38704
              depositum                  1201
   Do..............Cr.                   39905
By George West as p. accot.              1139
By 21 oe?. tobacco on 1046
   tithables                             39905
```

Mr. Charles Tyler dec.

(This appears to be a tithable list. For
each tithable the tax rate was 2.7.1/2.)
To Cash Rec'd from:

John Simms	2.7.1/2
Thos. Squire	7.1.1/2
John Dawson	5.3.
William Massey	2.7.1/2
John Peak	10.6.
John Queen	2.7.1/2
Frederick Whitmore	2.7.1/2
Charles Binns	5.3.
Jno. Goreham	2.7.1/2
	2.3.3
Excepted Jno. Craney	1.3

Mr. William Carr Lane   Dr.
To cash pd:

Aug. 13, 1765	
Mr. Craven Peyton as p. order	3.00.00
Sept. 10, 1765	
Revd. John Andrews	1.01.00
Benjamin Edwards	0.10.60
Sept. 15, 1765	
Fleming Patterson	7.02.11
Levin Powel	1.06.00
Josias Clapham	2.10.00
Stephen Donaldson	6.14.40
Augt. 13, 1766	
Thom: Mason Esq.	7.04.45
Samuel Conner	0.07.10
John Moss Sr.	0.18.40

Joseph Janny	0.02.70
William Mead	0.07.10
Aut. 13, 1765	
sent at Leesburg	0.01.00
Col. Minor	0.02.70
Doctor Broadbelt	0.02.70
Fleming Patterson & John Cavins	0.02.70
Col. Nicholas Minor	0.11.00
Patterson Par'h. levy	0.05.30
Edwd. Thompson	0.02.70
John Minor	0.10.60
Fleming Paterson	5.00.00
Charles Tyler late sherriff	2.03.30
Thomas Lewis do. sherrif	10.09.90
Fredrick Whitemore	0.02.70
George West pd. levys	0.13.10
Levin Powell leveys	<u>0.05.23</u>
	103.11.50

(The following appears exactly as it does in the suit. The colums heading are missing and there is no title. The second column appears to be tithables and right hand column appears to represent amounts of money.)

Daniel Conner	1	2.7.1/2
John Homes	1	2.7.1/2
Gregory Miller	1	2.7.1/2
George Russell	1	2.7.1/2
Peter Russell als.		
Roszell	2	5.3
Philip Senor	1	2.7.1/2
Wm. Vallandingham	3	7.10.12
John Smith	1	<u>2.7.1/2</u>
	11	1.8.10.1/2

Daniel Conner	1	2.7.1/2
(in Turners, below)		
John Crook	1	2.7.1/2
(in Geo. Wests)		
Philip Dowel	1	2.7.1/2
(in Mr. Nolands above)		
Joseph Ellis	1	2.7.1/2
(in Mr. Powels)		
John Homes	1	2.7.1/2
(Turners below)		
Gregorey Miller	1	2.7.1/2
(Turners below)		
John Mattox	1	2.7.1/2
~~Chas. Mobley~~	~~3~~	~~7.10.1/2~~
Daniel Moole	1	2.7.1/2
~~Wm. McRay~~	~~1~~	~~2.7.1/2~~
Patrick Maldeman	1	2.7.1/2
(Col. Hamiltons)		
Wm. Grimes	1	2.7.1/2
(Col. Minors)		
George Russel	1	2.7.1/2
(Paid Wm. Carr Lane)		
Peter Russel	2	5.3
(pd. Simon Turner)		
Phillip Venor	1	2.7.1/2
(Maj. Turners)		
James Sands	3	7.10.1/2
(Capt. Nolands)		
Wm. Valandingham	3	7.10.1/2
(Col. Minors)		
John Smith	1	2.7.1/2
(Maj. Turner)		
		1.8.10.1/2

(The following appears to be a list of
tithables. I have only included the
number of tithables, not the amount
paid. The tax rate was 2.7.1/2 for each
tithable.)

Awberry, Thomas	1
Austill, Isaac	2
Araqust, John	1
Arnot, Thomas	1
Adamson, Simon	1
Addison, William	1
Arthors, Joseph	2
Arris, John	1
Allin, William	1
Allin, John	1
Allin, Daniel	1
Allin, George	1
Anderson, Richard	1
Arnot, Alexd.	2
Adams, And.	6
Bogles, William	1
Bradley, Joseph	2
Batson, James	1
Baker, Nathanl.	1
Baker, William	3
Ball, John	1
Brooks, William	1
Barkley, Charles	1
Berrey, William	1
Baker, Phillip	1
Buffinton, James	1
Burson, Benja.	1
Bond, Thomas	2
Brooks, William	1
Ball, Failan	2
Brown, John	3

Brown, Henry	1
Belford, Daniel	2
Bradley, Joseph	1
Burk, John	1
Burnough, Wm.	4
Buckley, James	1
Bucklew, Richd.	4
Brown, John	1
Burson, George	2
Burson Jos. Mason	1
Burson, James	1
Burnes, Ignatious	1
Butcher, Saml.	1
Bucklew, Jonath.	1
Botts, Thomas	1
Baker, John	2
Bryan, Thomas	1
Boswall, Benj.	1
Butcher, John	1
Best, John	3
Brown, William	1
Brown, Mercer	1
Bishop, Saml.	1
Black, Wm.	1
Butlor?, Jas. B.belt	1
Barkley, Wm.	2
Burson, Benja.	1
Collins, John	1
Coleman, John	1
Connar, Danl.	1
Combs, Richd.	1
Cadwalader, Joseph	2
Clews, Thomas	3
Cumpson, Saml.	1
Cox, Joseph	1
Clapham, Josias	6

Carr, Thomas	1
Carr, John	2
Cargill, John	1
Conrad, Cornelious	1
Craig, Joseph	1
Collin, Wm.	1
Compton, Zebde	1
Conner, Saml.	3
Crook, John	1
Champe, John	2
Coldwell, Hugh	3
Chittarl, Mark	2
Connard, Jonathan	1
Coonts, Adam	1
Coomts, Henry	1
Craig, John	2
Craig, James	1
Clarkson, Wm.	1
Chinn, Charles	5
Chinn, Elijah	8
Combs, Joseph	6
Champe, Thomas	1
Clark, Benja.	2
Compton, Saml.	1
Cummins, Malacha	1
Cornelius, Wm.	1
Colemon, John	1
Carr, Walter	1
Coldwell, Joseph	1
Claypool, Joseph	2
Campbell, Rnes?	2
Combs, Saml.	2
Combs, John	1
Carter, James	1
Cornelius, Gerret	13
Carins, John	4
Christier, Philimon	1

Coopers, Frederick	1
Clerk, Francies	1
Davis, Jesse	1
Dowson, John	2
Dorf, Sam.	1
Davis, John	1
Donilson, Stephen	1
Dunkam, Epheram	1
Davis, John	1
Davis, Benja.	1
Davy, Jinkins	3
Deale, Saml.	1
Deale, Peter	1
Doley, Phillip	2
Davis, John	1
Dodd, Thomas	1
Dawkins, Saml.	1
Dodd, Wm.	2
Dowel, Phillip	1
Dawso?, Abraham	1
Davis, Cornelious	1
Dawkins, Wm.	3
Davis, Saml.	2
Davis, Saml. Jr.	1
Duncan, Joshua	1
Dillian, Josias	1
Dillian, Wm.	1
Dillian, James	2
Dunn, Joseph	1
Dexon, Soloman	2
Duncan, Saml.	2
Dye, Wm.	3
Dillian, Jonathan	1
Dillian, Jonathan	1
Dean, Saml.	1
Douglass, Wm.	11
Dixon, Wm.	1

Emrey, Stephen	1
Edward, Benja.	4
Ellgin, Frans.	3
Eaton, Henry Con.	1
Eddeman, James	1
Easton, James	1
Edwards, Joshua	1
Erwin, James	1
Eblind, John	1
Evans, John	1
Elis, Joseph	1
Fouch, Wm.	1
Fouch, John	1
Fouch, Isaac	1
Fouch, Hugh	2
Fouch, Jacob	1
Ferril, James o. Geo. West	1
Field, Thomas	8
Fielder, Wm.	1
Fout, Phillip	1
Fourgeson, Frans.	1
Frans. Lawrance	1
Faullan, Shadrick	1
Freeman, Richd.	1
Furr, Edwin?	1
French, Danl.	8
Furr, Ephram	2
Fowler, Wm.	1
Forguson, Henry	1
Fairfax, Geo. Wm. Col.	8
Fairhurst, Jerh.	2
Foruch, Abram	1
Gossel, Wm	2
Gardner, Joseph	4
Gore, Joshua	2
Gaws, Chas.	1
Gilland, James	1

Grant, John?	1
Green, Thomas	1
Grage, George	2
Gore, Thomas	2
Grider, Fredrick	2
Garret, David	1
Gregg, John	1
Garson, Nehemiah	3
Garison, Moses	2
Grigg, Thomas	2
Godwin, Amos	1
Gordin, Thomas	1
Grayson, Benj. P? Thonce?	14
Gosset, Matthias	1
Gore, John	1
Griffeth, John	1
Gorham, Thomas	1
Grimes, Wm.	1
Hatton, John	1
Hammond, Ephram	2
Holfield, Thos.	1
Hawkins, James	4
Hooten?, Thos.	1
Hares, Benja.	1
Howel, Timothy	2
Hickson, Matthew	1
Hickson, Wm.	1
Howel, John	1
Howel, John Jr.	1
Harby, John	1
Horse, Stuffell	1
Hopkins, Joseph	1
Harrison, Saml.	1
Howel, James	1
Holmes, Wm.	3
Hampton, Jerh.	1
Holden, John	2

Henderson, Thos.	1
Homes, John	1
Hernemus, Frans.	1
Humphres, Thos.	2
Harris, Wm.	1
Harris, David	1
Hollingworth, Elias	1
Hoof, Phillip	1
Hendrickson, John	1
Hamilton?, James	1
Henixon, Henry	11
Hill, Saml.	1
Henderson, Wm.	1
Hague, Solomon	1
Hague, Fran.	3
Hatcker, James	1
Hardie, Wm.	1
Holland, Patrick	1
Husher, Benja.	1
Howel, Hugh	2
Hamilton, Robert	1
Hunt, Danl.	1
Hudson, Richd.	1
Howell, John	1
Hamard, Wm.	1
Hatcher, Wm.	3
Haraford, John	3
Hunt, James	1
Hame, Christan	1
Hatcher, John	1
Haitherly, John	1
Hague, John	1
Hough, John	4
Hoge, Wm.	2
Hoge, Wm. Jr.	1
Havin, Howard	1
Hutton, Joseph	1

Henderson, James	1
Hugne, Isaac	1
Hoofman, Jacob	1
Havin, John	1
Hallfield, Edward	1
Hate, Nathan	1
Hibbs, Isaac	1
Hanke, Wm.	1
Hough, Benja.	2
Hough, Henry	1
Johnson, Wm.	1
Jones, Danl.	1
Janney, Joseph	1
Jones, John	4
Jenniscs, Mary	2
Jenney, Mahlon	3
Jenney, Abel	2
Iden, Saml.	1
Jackson, Thomas	1
Jones, Joseph	2
Jones, Thomas	1
Jones, Theophalus	1
Jackson, Wm.	2
Jones, Abraham	1
Jones, John	1
Jackson, Henry	1
Jackson, Alexis	1
Janney, Jacob B. Smith	4
Jlere, Jacob	1
Jones, Thomas	1
Jones, Wm.	3
Janney, Wm.	4
James, John	1
Kester, Wm.	1
Kidwallit, Moses	1
Kidwallit, John	1
Kirk, Wm.	2

Kiger, John	1
Kelly, Thomas	1
King, Richd.	1
Lumb, Thomas	2
Lacock, Wm.	1
Lewis, Thomas	1
Lawrance, Danl.	1
Lewis, John	1
Lannon, Joseph	1
Lewis, Charles	1
Lewis, Stephen	1
Lewis, George	2
Long, James	2
Long, George	2
Lister, John	3
Leveling, Thos.	2
Little, John	2
Leith, James	2
Lynn, Matthews	1
Laycock, Nathan	1
Lewis, John	1
Miller, Gregory	1
McColley, Thos.	1
Munkhouse, Jonathan	3
Moore, Benja.	1
Mullings, John	1
Merrich, Griffeth	2
McGinnis, John	1
Mason, Tomson, Esq.	55
Minor, Nicholas	1
Minor, John	2
Mead, Wm.	3
Moss, Peter	1
Massey, Abraham	1
Murrey, James	1
Moss, John Sr.	5
Massey, Lee	8

Morriss, John	1
Mattox, John	1
Massay, Lewis	1
Mollon, Wm.	1
Massey, Wm.	1
McHany, John	4
McManamy, Chas.	1
Marrs, Jonathan	1
Martin, Ralph	2
Martin, Wm. son of Ralph	1
Mutheny, Danl.	1
Moore, Elnothan	1
Martin, Andrew	1
McNanamy, John	1
Martin, Joseph	1
Matheny, Nathan	1
Matheny, Wm. Jr.	1
Mead, Saml.	4
Mobby, Charles	3
Megrews, Chas.	1
McKenney, Patrick	1
Middleton, Walter	2
Middleton, Holland Jr.	1
Middleton, Thos. Jr.	1
Middleton, Holland	2
McMillion, John	1
Munroe, Geo.	1
McPhierson, Richd.	2
McBerry, Frans.	2
Mercer, James	12
McChristy, Arther	1
McKnight, Wm.	1
Marks, John	2
Moole, Danl.	1
McDonald, John	1
Miller, John	2
McCay, Wm.	1

McAldimer, Patrick	1
Marknoal, Wm.	1
McFarling, Wm.	1
Middleton, Thos.	1
Nixon, James	1
Nicoldson, Jereh.	1
Nichols, Christ.	1
Nealson, Richd.	1
Noland, Philip	2
Nichols, James	1
Nichols, Isaac	2
Norman, George	1
Neighbour, Nath.	1
Nichols, James	1
Norton, John	1
Oliver, John	1
Oxley, Henry	4
Oxley, Henry Jr.	2
Oxley, Averest	1
Oxley, John	1
Owsley, Pines	1
Owsley, John Dueat	1
Owsley, Thos.	3
Owsley, Newdijate	2
Oneal Fardenanda	3
Osborn, John	7
Odaniel, Henry	1
Phan, Jacob	1
Perfect, Christ.	1
Popkins, Robt.	2
Prickard, Thos.	4
Pool, Benja.	1
Posham, Leonard	1
Peak, John	4
Potton, Henry	1
Peyton, Craven	8
Potts, Jonathan	1

Potts, Saml.	1
Potts, David	3
Peason, Saml.	1
Potts, Jonas	1
Pursley, Thos.	2
Pendam, Benja.	1
Priece, Evan	2
Phillips, Thos.	1
Paterson, Wm.	3
Peyton, Frans.	8
Powel, Levin	2
Pearl, Wm. Jr.	1
Peyton, Robt.	4
Power, Joseph	1
Preston, Isaac	1
Phillips, James	3
Palmer, Jonathan	1
Palmer, John	1
Phillips, Ezil?	1
Pratt, Jerh.	1
Phillips, Jinkin	2
Phillips, Saml.	1
Phillips, Thos.	2
Palmer, Danl.	1
Pearce, John	1
hillips, Thos.	3
Potts, John	3
Pavel, Richd.	1
Peterson, John	2
Qick, Casher	1
Queen, John	1
Russell, Peter	2
Ross, James	2
Russuel, Saml.	1
Rame, John	1
Rhodes, Moses	1
Reeger?, John	1

Roach, Richd.	1
Richardson, Jonth.	1
Rees, Lewis	1
Roxal, Davis	1
Rogers, Nicolas	1
Right, Henry	1
Rredman, James	3
Russell, Chas.	2
Robinson, Elisha	2
Reed, Jacob	2
Rust, Wm.	3
Robin, Joshua	2
Romine, Peter	3
Ray, Thomas	1
Redikin, Patrick	2
Russell, Geo.	1
Scanor, Phillip	1
Spencer, Nathan	1
Sreve, Benja.	1
Sorrill, Thos.	5
Shilling, Jacob	1
Shilton, Fran.	1
Shepherd, James	1
Smith, Nathaniel	3
Stephens, Giles	2
Squres, Thos.	3
Shores, Thos.	6
Squres, John	1
Stroud, Saml.	1
Shoemaker, Danl.	1
Shoemaker, Peter	1
Shoemaker, George	1
Sedake, John	1
Schooley, Saml.	2
Schooley, John	1
Scott, Henry	1
Shomaker, Jacob	2

Shaven, John	1
Swing, Danl.	1
Shavirges	1
Shomaker, Simon	1
Swing, John	1
Smith, Wm.	1
Swellback, And.	1
Stillwell, Saml.	2
Sams, Ednear?	1
Swiger, Christ.	1
Sands, Edmond	3
Shepard, Thos.	2
Sinkler, John	3
Sands, James	3
Smith, David	3
Steer, John	2
Steer, James	1
Scott, John	1
Smithyman, Saml.	1
Shrewsberry, Thos.	1
Saunders, Moses	1
Settle, Josias	1
Saunders, Isaac	1
Simms, John	1
Simpson, Gilbert	4
Stark, Thos.	1
Saunders, Aaron	1
Smith, Wm.	3
Saunders, Geo.	1
Shepard, Thos.	1
Symbole, Jas. Jr.	1
Sreve, John	1
Smith, Saml.	4
Stump, Thos.	2
Sreve, Caleb	2
Schooley, Wm.	1
Sheperd, John	1

Smith, John	1
Tompson, Edward	1
Thomas, John	2
Tillet, Saml.	3
Trenary, Richd.	1
Tohick, Hanie John	1
Tohick, Henry	2
Teel, Phillip	1
Tavener, Richd.	1
Taylor, Henry	7
Tompson, Isreal	10
Tobine, Thos.	1
Trop?, Henry	1
Thomas, James	1
Taylor, Jam.?	1
Tryby, Jam.	1
Thomas, John	1
Trammel, John	1
Taylor, Edwd.	1
Taylor, Wm.	2
Triplett, Wm.	3
Triplett, Thos.	2
Triplett, Danl.	2
Taylor, ???	4
Thatcher, Michl.	2
Trudget, Wm.	1
Tompson, Thoms.	1
Tankervill Erl.	7
Thomas, Jonathan	2
Updike, John	1
Vess, Wm.	1
Vallandingham, Wm.	3
Vallandingham, Wm.	1
Vanbuscart, John	1
Vanbuscart, Isaac	1
Vanbuscart, Mich.	1
Voyle, John	1

Vincent, Isaac	1
Wilks, Jrrane???	1
Wilks, Saml.	1
Williams, Wm.	1
White, Richd.	3
Wilks, John	1
Willson, Joseph	1
Wigmire, John Frederick	1
Wedouer, Alexander	1
Wirt, Jas.	2
Williamson, James	1
Williamson, Potety	1
Wyat, Thomas	1
Wildman, Wm	2
Walter, Conrad	1
Wimsel, Adam	1
Wyat, John	1
Warford, John	1
Williams, David	1
Weeser, Fredrick	1
Wiggins, Rob.	1
Williams, Richd.	3
Whiteley, Wm.	3
Wood, Elias	1
Williams, Thomas	3
Whilock, James	2
Williams, Walter	2
Woolard, Wm.	1
Wood, Jos.	1
West, Edward	1
Willson, Joshua	2
Whitacer, John	3
Whitacer, John Jr.	1
Whitacer, Ignatious	2
Warford, Joseph	1
Williams, Enock	1
Wood, Isaac	1

Walter, Isaac	2
Walton, John	1
West, George	4
Yelding, Robt.	1
Yates, Alice	1
Yates, Joshua	1

Pursuant to an order of Loudoun Coty. to determine a controvery depending between Wm. Carr Lane & George West, Gent. Churchwardens of Cameron Parish defs. agst. John Evans, Jas. Hamilton, and John Andrews, clerk defts - upon examining the accts. on each side do award and determine that the Plts. recover agst. the defts. the sum of 29 pounds, 12 shillings. and 2 pence half penny together with interest from the 25th of December 1765 till payment. Sept. 13, 1771.

Chas. Binns
Thos. Lewis

Sept. 14, 1771. Award ret'd. & Judgm't. for 29.121.2 1/2 & interest from the 25th Dec. 1765 till paid and abated as the deft. Andrews being dead.

(The following entries were found in order books B & C of Loudoun County, Virginia pertaining to Cameron Parish from 1762-67.)

B:77. Dec. 14, 1762. Christain Woodhouse a servant belonging to Minor

Winn was brought before Court by her master for having a base born child, Withers Smith is father, she forfiet and pay 50 shilling, or 500 pounds of tob. to Churchwardens of Cameron Parish.

B:91. April 13, 1763 Francis Peyton & Charles Tylor vs Barbary Remey in debt. The Deft. being again returned not found on motion of Plts. issue plurius capias is awarded then returnable here at next Court.

B:212. Aug. 11, 1763. Nicholas Minor and Francis Peyton vs Elizabeth Grantham, in debt. Matters therein contained are not good & suifficient in law from Plt to have their action ag't. deft. therefore plt. take nothing by their bill.
B:213. Date same. Nicholas Minor & Fracnis Peyton Churchwardens of Cameron Parish vs Mary Martin, in debt. Plts. take nothing by their bill.

B:215. Aug. 12, 1763. Charles Tyler & Francis Peyton, Gent. Churchwardens for time of Parish of Cameron vs Rachel Hall, upon an information. Discontinued, the Plt. not further prosecuting.

B:222. Aug. 12, 1763. Nicholas Minor & Leonard Dozer Churchwardens of Cameron Parish vs. Sarah Pritchard in debt. Discontinued, not further prosecuting.

B:290. March 15, 1764. Upon petition from Francis Peyton & Nicholas Minor Churchwardens of Cameron Parish who sue for use of parish ag't. Mary Windsor for a debt due by judg't. of Loudoun Co. Court this day came the Plt. by Hugh West their attorney, deft. came not. Therefore is is considered by Court that Plt. recover ag't. Deft. 500 lbs. of tob. & cost or 50 shilling curr. money, 146 lbs. of tob., 15 shilling or 150 lbs. tob., also cost.

B:488. Oct. 10, 1764. John Moss produced a certificate from Vestry of Cameron Parish wherein it appears that he was chosen by the minister & majority of the Vestry to be a Vestryman in the room of Charles Binn who resigned & thereupon
he took the oaths to his Majesties person & government and subscribes to be conformable to the doctrine of Discipline of the Church of England.

C:212. Oct. 15, 1766. Charles Tyler & John Moss, Gent. Churchwardens of Cameron Parish vs Jane Jew in debt. Discontinued.

C:239. March 10, 1767. John Moss & Charles Tyler vs Sarah Matheny in debt, suit dismissed being agreed.

C:248. April 15, 1767. Charles Tyler & John Moss vs Elizabeth Stoker, debt. Suit discontinued, def. being no inhabitant.

Carr, Thomas, 9
Carr, Walter, 9
Carter, James, 9
Carlyle
  John, 2
Cavins
  John, 5
Champe, John, 9
Champe, Thomas, 9
Chinn, Charles, 9
Chinn, Elijah, 9
Chittarl, Mark, 9
Christier, Philimon, 9
Clapham
  Josias, 2, 4
Clapham, Josias, 8
Clark, Benja., 9
Clarkson, Wm., 9
Claypool, Joseph, 9
Clerk, Francies, 10
Clews, Thomas, 8
Coldwell, Hugh, 9
Coldwell, Joseph, 9
Coleman
  Elinor, 3
Coleman, John, 8
Colemon, John, 9
Collin, Wm., 9
Collins, John, 8
Combs, John, 9
Combs, Joseph, 9
Combs, Richd., 8
Combs, Saml., 9
Compton, Saml., 9
Compton, Zebde, 9
Connar, Danl., 8
Connard, Jonathan, 9

Conner
  Daniel, 5, 6
  Samuel, 4
Conner, Saml., 9
Conrad, Cornelious, 9
Coomts, Henry, 9
Coonts, Adam, 9
Coopers, Frederick, 10
Cornelius, Gerret, 9
Cornelius, Wm., 9
Cox, Joseph, 8
Craig, James, 9
Craig, John, 9
Craig, Joseph, 9
Craney
  Jno., 4
Crook
  John, 6, 9
Cummins, Malacha, 9
Cumpson, Saml., 8

D
Davis, Benja., 10
Davis, Cornelious, 10
Davis, Jesse, 10
Davis, John, 10
Davis, Saml., 10
Davis, Saml. Jr., 10
Davy, Jinkins, 10
Dawkins, Saml., 10
Dawkins, Wm., 10
Dawso?, Abraham, 10
Dawson
  John, 4
Deale, Peter, 10
Deale, Saml., 10
Dean, Saml., 10

Dexon, Soloman, 10
Dillian, James, 10
Dillian, Jonathan, 10
Dillian, Josias, 10
Dillian, Wm., 10
Dixon, Wm., 10
Dodd, Thomas, 10
Dodd, Wm., 10
Doley, Phillip, 10
Donaldson/Donilson
    Stephen, 4, 10
Dorf, Sam., 10
Douglass, Wm., 10
Dowel
    Philip, 6, 10
Dowson, John, 10
Dozer
    Leonard, 24
Duncan, Joshua, 10
Duncan, Saml., 10
Dunkam, Epheram, 10
Dunn, Joseph, 10
Dye, Wm., 10

E
Easton, James, 11
Eaton, Henry Con., 11
Eblind, John, 11
Eddeman, James, 11
Edwards
    Benjamin, 4, 11
Edwards, Joshua, 11
Elis, Joseph, 11
Ellgin, Frans., 11
Ellis
    Joseph, 6
Emrey, Stephen, 11

Leith, James, 15
Leveling, Thos., 15
Lewis
   Charles, 15
   George, 15
   John, 2, 15
   Stephen, 15
   Thomas, 5, 15
   Thos., 2, 23
Lister, John, 15
Little River, 1
Little, John, 15
Long, George, 15
Long, James, 15
Lumb, Thomas, 15
Lynn, Matthews, 15

M
Maldeman
   Patrick, 6
Marknoal, Wm., 17
Marks, John, 16
Marrs, Jonathan, 16
Martin, Andrew, 16
Martin, Joseph, 16
Martin, Mary 24
Martin, Ralph, 16
Martin, Wm. son of Ralph, 16
Mason
   Thom., 4
Mason, Tomson, Esq., 15
Massey, Abraham, 15
Massey, Lee, 15
Massay, Lewis, 16
Massey, Wm., 16
Massey, William 4

Miller
  Gregory, 5, 6, 15
Miller, John, 16
Milton
  James, 1
Minor
  Col., 5, 6
  Col. Nicholas, 5
  John, 5
  Nicholas, 15, 24, 25
Minor, John, 15
Mobby, Charles, 16
Mobley
  Chas., 6
Mollon, Wm., 16
Moole
  Daniel, 6
Moole, Danl., 16
Moore, Benja., 15
Moore, Elnothan, 16
Morriss, John, 16
Moss
  John, 3, 25
  John Jr., 2
  John Sr., 4, 15
  Peter, 15
Mountian Church, 2
Mullings, John, 15
Munkhouse, Jonathan, 15
Munroe, Geo., 16
Murrey, James, 15
Mutheny, Danl., 16

N
Nealson, Richd., 17
Neighbour, Nath., 17
Nichols, Christ., 17

T

Tankervill Erl., 21
Tavener, Richd., 21
Taylor, Edwd., 21
Taylor, Jam., 21
Taylor, Henry, 21
Taylor, Jam.?, 21
Taylor, Wm., 21
Teel, Phillip, 21
Thatcher, Michl., 21
Thomas, James, 21
Thomas, John, 21
Thomas, Jonathan, 21
Thompson/see Tompson
   Edwd., 3, 5
Tillet, Saml., 21
Tobine, Thos., 21
Tohick, Hanie John, 21
Tohick, Henry, 21
Tompson, Edward, 21
Tompson, Isreal, 21
Tompson, Thoms., 21
Trammel, John, 21
Trenary, Richd., 21
Triplett, Danl., 21
Triplett, Thos., 21
Triplett, Wm., 21
Trop, Henry, 21
Trudget, Wm., 21
Tryby, Jam., 21
Turner, 6
   Maj., 6
   Simon, 6
Tyler
   Charles, 2, 4, 5, 24, 25

Wigmire, John Frederick, 22
Wildman, Wm, 22
Wilks, John, 22
Wilks, Jrrane???, 22
Wilks, Saml., 22
Williams, David, 22
Williams, Enock, 22
Williams, Richd., 22
Williams, Thomas, 22
Williams, Walter, 22
Williams, Wm., 22
Williamson, James, 22
Williamson, Potety, 22
Willson
  Henry, 2
Willson, Joseph, 22
Willson, Joshua, 22
Wimsel, Adam, 22
Windsor
  Mary, 25
Winn
  Minor, 24
  William, 3
Wirt, Jas., 22
Wood, Elias, 22
Wood, Isaac, 22
Wood, Jos., 22
Woodhouse
  Christain, 23
Woolard, Wm., 22
Wyat, John, 22
Wyat, Thomas, 22

Y
Yates, Alice, 23
Yates, Joshua, 23
Yelding, Robt., 23

www.ingramcontent.com/pod-product-compliance
Lightning Source LLC
Chambersburg PA
CBHW051711090426
42736CB00013B/2656